LEARN TO DRAW

DREAMWORKS

SHREK THE THIRD

Illustrated by
Shane L. Johnson

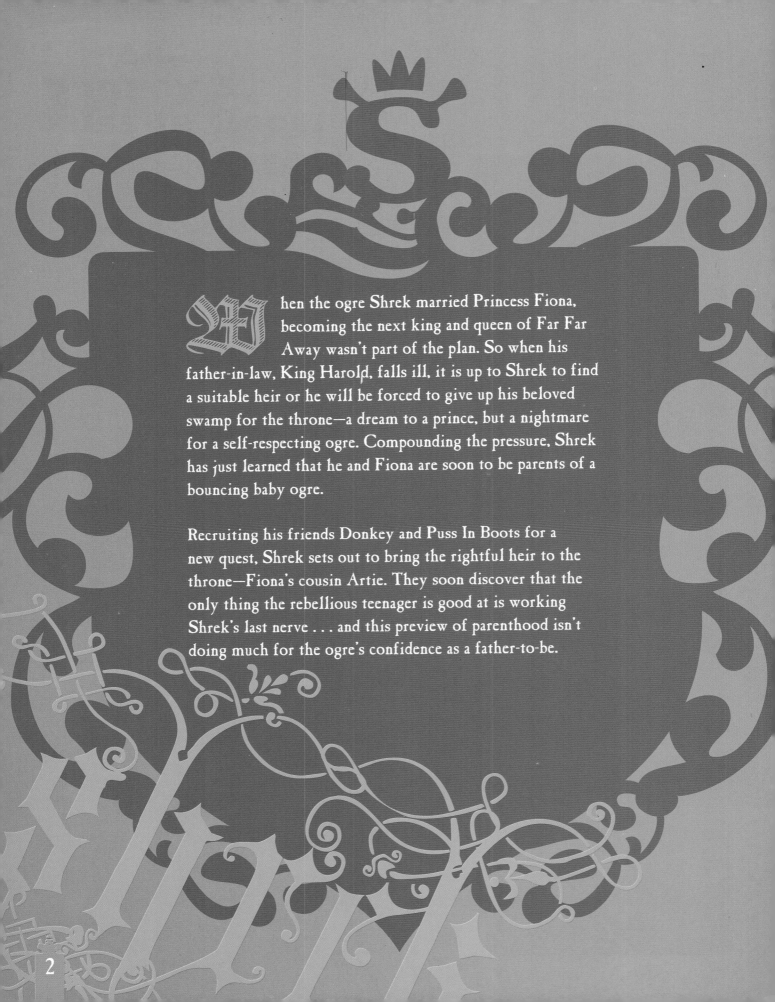

When the ogre Shrek married Princess Fiona, becoming the next king and queen of Far Far Away wasn't part of the plan. So when his father-in-law, King Harold, falls ill, it is up to Shrek to find a suitable heir or he will be forced to give up his beloved swamp for the throne—a dream to a prince, but a nightmare for a self-respecting ogre. Compounding the pressure, Shrek has just learned that he and Fiona are soon to be parents of a bouncing baby ogre.

Recruiting his friends Donkey and Puss In Boots for a new quest, Shrek sets out to bring the rightful heir to the throne—Fiona's cousin Artie. They soon discover that the only thing the rebellious teenager is good at is working Shrek's last nerve . . . and this preview of parenthood isn't doing much for the ogre's confidence as a father-to-be.

Back in Far Far
Away, Fiona's jilted
Prince Charming seizes his chance
to claim the throne, storming the city
with an army of fairy-tale villains. But
they have a surprise in store because Fiona,
together with her mother, Queen Lillian,
has drafted her fellow fairy-tale heroines
to defend their Happily Ever Afters.

As Shrek, Donkey, and Puss work on changing Artie
from a royal pain in the you-know-what into a once and
future king, Fiona and her band of princesses must stop
Prince Charming and ensure there will be a kingdom
left to rule.

Tools & Materials

In this book, you'll learn how to draw your favorite *Shrek the Third* characters. All you need are a few simple tools to get started on your masterpieces! Begin with a pencil (like the one you use in school), an eraser, and a pencil sharpener. When you're done with your drawing, you can add color with colored pencils, crayons, markers, or even acrylic or watercolor paints. The choice is up to you!

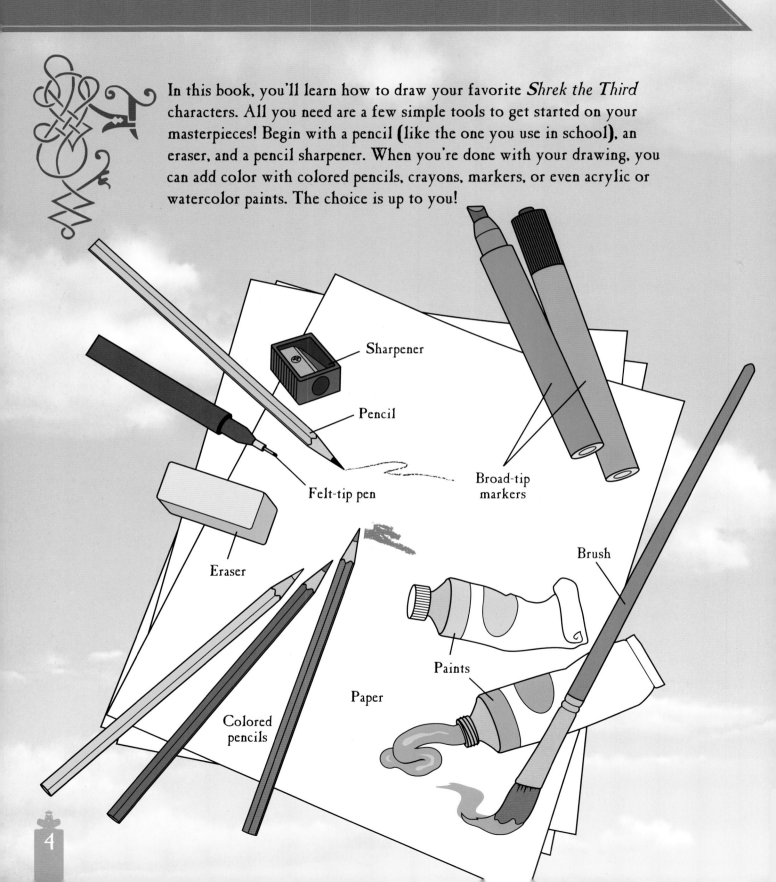

Sharpener

Pencil

Felt-tip pen

Broad-tip markers

Brush

Eraser

Paints

Paper

Colored pencils

How to Use This Book

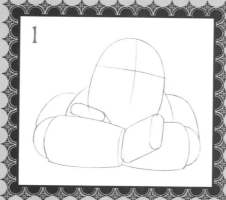

Start your drawing by blocking in basic shapes and adding guidelines.

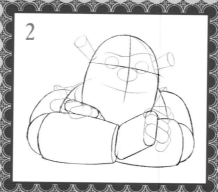

Each new step appears in blue, so you'll always know what to draw next!

Simply follow the blue lines to add each new feature.

Refine your drawing by adding all the details.

Darken the lines you want to keep and erase the rest.

Use bright, bold colors to make your characters pop off the paper!

Character Lineup

When animators draw, they pay close attention to a character's *proportions* (or the sizes of things compared with other things around them). Humans, ogres, and animals are often measured in "heads." For example, Shrek is about 3-1/2 heads tall. As you draw, use this handy guide to check the characters' heights and proportions.

5

4

3

2

1

SHREK

Shrek's head is egg shaped—narrow at the top and wide at the bottom.

Don't be misled by Shrek's green skin, yellow teeth, and burly shape—there is a lot more to this ogre than meets the eye! Shrek may look scary and even mean, but he's a kindhearted soul who enjoys the simple things in life, like taking slimy mud showers and spending quiet time with his new wife, Fiona.

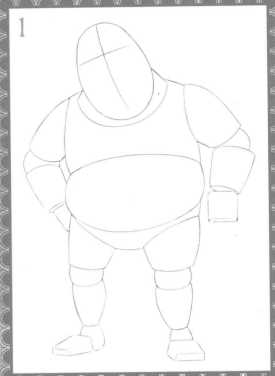

The basic structure can be broken down into blocks and cylinders. Shrek is a 3-D character, so think in 3-D as you draw him.

The base of both Shrek's eyes and ears line up with the top of his nose!

2

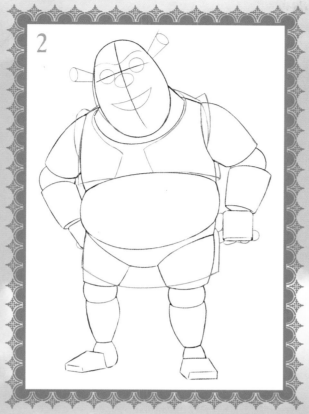

3

5

6

DONKEY

Donkey's motor mouth has gotten him into trouble in the past, but it's the least of his worries these days. Now that he's married Dragon, Donkey has a whole litter of little Dronkeys to occupy his time—that is, when Shrek doesn't need him to trot off on an adventure.

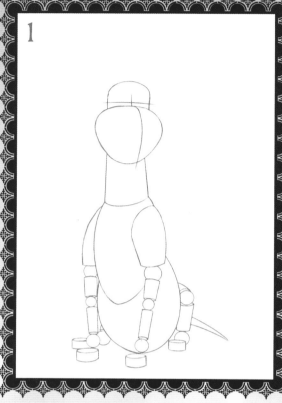

1

4

Donkey's ears are shaped like bananas.

Donkey is furry, but you don't need to draw every hair on him! Just add big tufts on the top of his head and tip of his tail.

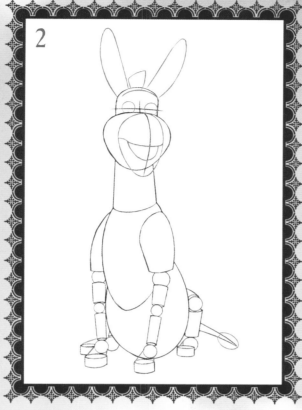

2

3

5

6

Fiona's hair makes her head oval in shape; but her face itself is round, like a ball.

Princess Fiona is not your typical damsel in distress. She's smart, tough, and has been known to dropkick a band of outlaws.

1

4

12

You don't see Fiona's legs, but you should still draw them. "Drawing through" will help you position the feet. (You can erase the extra lines later.)

Fiona has a cute button nose. Draw one big circle with a small oval on each side.

2

3

5

6

Puss In Boots

Despite his sweet appearance, this suave kitty cat makes one strong side-kick. Not only does he bravely lend Shrek a hand whenever he's in need, Puss also reminds his ogre friend how things look from a bachelor's point of view!

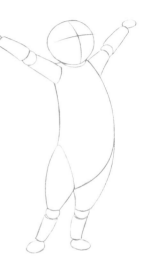

1

4

Remember, Puss is a cat, and cats' pupils are slivers, not circles.

Puss is never without these essential items: stylish hat, buccaneering belt, miniature sword, and leather boots.

2

3

5

6

Fiona & Shrek

Although he married a princess, the royal life isn't for Shrek. These newly-weds are ready to escape the hectic life of the kingdom so that they can live out their days quietly in their swamp home.

1

4

These ogres have their differences, but Fiona's eyes, ears, and nose line up just like Shrek's do!

There is a little space between Shrek's nose and mouth—but draw too much distance, and he'll look like a chimpanzee!

Shrek, Donkey & Puss In Boots

The outer rims of Shrek's ears are triangles with rounded edges.

This inseparable trio can't seem to leave behind adventure—or trouble, for that matter! Their latest quest is to bring back the next heir to the throne of Far Far Away.

1

4

The top of Donkey's head is rectangular in shape. His circular muzzle becomes oval when opened—which is often.

The stem of Puss's feather plume comes through his hat brim.

ARTIE

Arthur "Artie" Pendragon is Fiona's cousin and the next heir to the throne. At first he's not interested in ruling Far Far Away, but in the end he finds the crown fits him quite well.

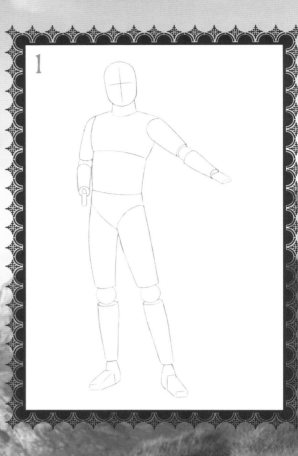

1

4

The tops of Artie's nose and ears start halfway down his face. Place the other features accordingly.

Artie's big mop of messy hair makes his head seem bigger—and his face look scrawnier!

2

3

5

6

Prince Charming

Prince Charming has a handsome face, with a square jaw, a chiseled nose, and wide-set eyes.

Prince Charming is a mama's boy at heart. But his mama, Fairy Godmother, couldn't give him what he really wanted—the Far Far Away kingdom. Charming enlists the help of the fairy-tale villains in hopes of becoming king and getting his Happily Ever After.

1

4

He's more than just a mama's boy—he's a pretty boy too. That explains his perfectly coifed, center-parted hairdo.

 Charming's shoulders are wide and square. His chest is likewise broad and muscular.

Merlin

A retired high-school magic teacher, all Merlin really wants is to be left in peace. Yet he stills employs his rusty magic to help Shrek and his friends when they are in need.

1

4

 Merlin's head is oval, but the visible part of his face is round, as are his glasses and nose.

 Wrinkles above the magician's brow and around his eyes help show his age.

2

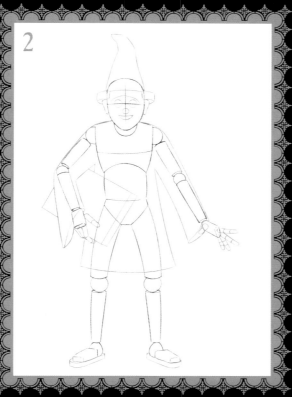

3

5

6

Pinocchio & Gingy

Thrown together by fate, this wooden boy and gingerbread man have become the best of friends. They act as Shrek's house-sitters—and his rescuers!

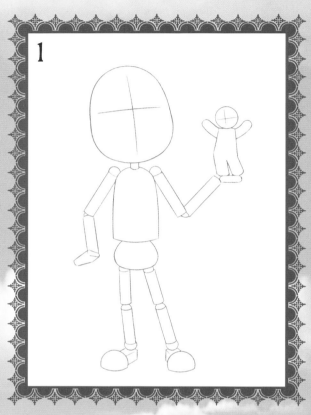

1

4

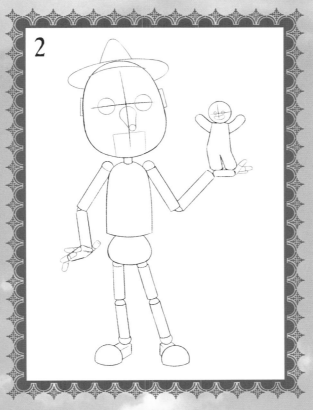

Wolf & Pigs

The Pigs' noses are shaped like a pentagon. They have five points.

Part of the fairy-tale posse, Wolf and The Three Pigs have become close friends of Shrek and Fiona! Like the fairy-tale princesses, Wolf and the Pigs join the battle against Prince Charming in his quest for the throne.

1

4

Wolf's teeth are sharp but not too big—when it comes down to it, he's really not *that* big and bad!

Each little Pig wears its own hat, but their faces and bodies are the same! From the side, each Pig has a long snout with a small bump on top.

2

3

5

6

Captain Hook

Hook was recruited by Prince Charming at The Poison Apple. Haunted by bad memories of his experience with Peter Pan, Hook is determined to claim his Happily Ever After.

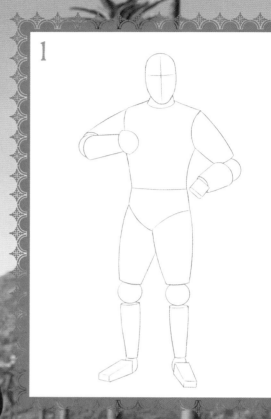

1

4

This villain has a boxy chin and a large hooked nose that's quite fitting for his name!

Cyclops

As doorman, it's Cyclops' job to keep an eye on the black-hearted rogues and scoundrels who frequent The Poison Apple pub.

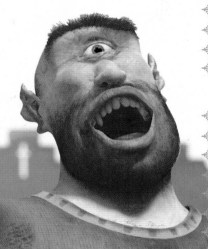

1

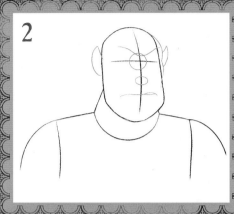

2

3

4

5

6